This address book belongs to

NAME: . . . .

ADDRESS: . . . .

. . . .

. . . .

TEL: . . . .

FAX: . . . .

EMAIL: . . . .

Tibetan Spaniel, Florence Jay

DOG PAINTING

A history of the dog in art

ADDRESS BOOK

ANTIQUE COLLECTORS' CLUB

ISBN 978 1 85149 617 4

British Library Cataloguing-in-Publication Data
A catalogue record for this book is available from the British Library

Frontispiece: Setters and a Spaniel, Richard Ansdell
Title page: Wire Fox Terrier, Arthur Wardle

Printed in China
for the Antique Collectors' Club Ltd., Woodbridge, Suffolk

Foreword

Nineteenth century paintings of dogs have been of interest to pure-bred dog fanciers for decades. In the last ten years or so, however, they have come to the attention of a new and appreciative public.

Whether depicting a highly bred canine, a sporting dog in the field or a beloved pet, the appeal of dog paintings is obvious. They strike a responsive chord in all of us, for even if we need to reach back into the early years of our childhood, there are few of us indeed who have not been touched by the love of a dog.

Over the last few years I have noticed a significant change in collectors' attitudes towards dog paintings. What were once viewed as historical documents illustrating the history of a breed, are now being recognised as works of art.

The paintings in this address book are selected from the comprehensive volume, *Dog Painting: A History of the Dog in Art*, and represent only a few of the wide variety of breeds and fine artists to be found among this increasingly popular genre.

William Secord
President
William Secord Gallery, Inc.
New York

Clumber Spaniels, Reuben Ward Binks

Dog Painting: a history of the dog in art

All the illustrations in this book have been taken from the Antique Collectors' Club publication *Dog Painting: a history of the dog in art* by William Secord. This magnificent volume is a testament to man's affection for our canine friends, depicted in art since before the birth of Christ, emerging triumphantly in nineteenth century England, Europe and America.

With wit and enthusiasm, William Secord tells the story of the origins and development of dog painting and explains the various forces which emerged in 19th century England and America to create this golden age of dog painting.

Richly illustrated in full colour with over 525 paintings, *Dog Painting: a history of the dog in art* is a visual delight as well as an important and invaluable reference work not only of the changing breeds through history, but also of the many superb painters who specialised in dog painting.

To order your copy now please contact:

www.antiquecollectorsclub.com

Antique Collectors' Club
Sandy Lane, Old Martlesham
Woodbridge, Suffolk IP12 4SD, UK
Tel: 01394 389950 Fax: 01394 389999
Email: info@antique-acc.com

ACC Distribution
6 West 18th Street,
4th Floor, New York, NY, 10011, USA
Tel: (800) 252 5231
Email: orders@antiquecc.com

About this book

An address book faithfully preserves the details of cherished friends as well as useful contacts, both sources of amusement and duty. It is thus comparable to that symbol of fidelity and trust throughout the ages: man's best friend, servant and dependable ally – the dog.

The publishers would like to thank Bill Secord for writing his wonderful book *Dog Painting* and for allowing them to use some of the illustrations in this address book.

Dogs are illustrated in many different moods and environments, enlivening the pages with the colourful character of dozens of breeds, each with its own attraction and purpose, whether for sport or for show, for domestic use or simply as an adored pet. Comparison of paintings of a particular breed also enable the changes in its development over the years to be traced.

These portraits give pleasure as well as relief to the steady record of names, places and numbers every human life accumulates.

It is hoped that for many years this book will give pleasure to people who love dogs.

Newfoundland and Leonberger, Elizabeth Sinding

Important telephone numbers

DOCTOR: . . . .   POLICE: . . . .

DENTIST: . . . .   BUILDER: . . . .

VET: . . . .   PLUMBER: . . . .

ELECTRICITY: . . . .   GAS: . . . .

WATER: . . . .   TELEPHONE: . . . .

BANK: . . . .   INSURANCE: . . . .

GARAGE: . . . .   TAXI: . . . .

. . . .

. . . .

. . . .

. . . .

. . . .

. . . .

. . . .

Spaniel, Abraham Cooper

NAME...

ADDRESS ....

....

....

....

TEL ....

MOBILE ....

E-MAIL ....

NAME...

ADDRESS ....

....

....

....

TEL ....

MOBILE ....

E-MAIL ....

A

Skye Terrier, Gourlay Steell

NAME ....

ADDRESS ....
....
....
....
....

TEL ....
MOBILE ....
E-MAIL ....

NAME ....
....
ADDRESS ....
....
....
....
....

TEL ....
MOBILE ....
E-MAIL ....

NAME ....
....
ADDRESS ....
....
....
....
....

TEL ....
MOBILE ....
E-MAIL ....

NAME ....

ADDRESS ....
....
....
....
....

TEL ....
MOBILE ....
E-MAIL ....

NAME ....
....
ADDRESS ....
....
....
....
....

TEL ....
MOBILE ....
E-MAIL ....

B

NAME...
....
ADDRESS ....
....
....
....
....
TEL ....
MOBILE ....
E-MAIL ....

NAME...
....
ADDRESS ....
....
....
....
....
TEL ....
MOBILE ....
E-MAIL ....

Collies, Wright Barker

B

Dandie Dinmont, George Earl

NAME ....

ADDRESS ....

....

....

....

....

TEL ....
MOBILE ....
E-MAIL ....

NAME ....

....

ADDRESS ....

....

....

....

....

TEL ....
MOBILE ....
E-MAIL ....

NAME ....

....

ADDRESS ....

....

....

....

....

TEL ....
MOBILE ....
E-MAIL ....

NAME ....

....

ADDRESS ....

....

....

....

....

TEL ....
MOBILE ....
E-MAIL ....

NAME ....

....

ADDRESS ....

....

....

....

....

TEL ....
MOBILE ....
E-MAIL ....

NAME..

....

ADDRESS ....

....

....

....

....

TEL ....

MOBILE ....

E-MAIL ....

NAME..

....

ADDRESS ....

....

....

....

....

TEL ....

MOBILE ....

E-MAIL ....

NAME..

....

ADDRESS ....

....

....

....

....

TEL ....

MOBILE ....

E-MAIL ....

NAME..

....

ADDRESS ....

....

....

....

....

TEL ....

MOBILE ....

E-MAIL ....

NAME..

....

ADDRESS ....

....

....

....

....

TEL ....

MOBILE ....

E-MAIL ....

Cairn Terrier, Maud Earl

B

NAME...
....
ADDRESS ....
....
....
....
....
TEL ....
MOBILE ....
E-MAIL ....

NAME...
....
ADDRESS ....
....
....
....
....
TEL ....
MOBILE ....
E-MAIL ....

NAME...
....
ADDRESS ....
....
....
....
....
TEL ....
MOBILE ....
E-MAIL ....

NAME...
....
ADDRESS ....
....
....
....
....
TEL ....
MOBILE ....
E-MAIL ....

Bulldogs, Anna Maria Stork-Kruyff

NAME...
....
ADDRESS ....
....
....
....
....
TEL ....
MOBILE ....
E-MAIL ....

Dogs have given us their absolute all. We are the centre of their universe. We are the focus of their love and faith and trust. They serve us in return for scraps. It is without a doubt the best deal man has ever made. Roger Caras

NAME...
....
ADDRESS ....
....
....
....
....
TEL ....
MOBILE ....
E-MAIL ....

NAME...
....
ADDRESS ....
....
....
....
....
TEL ....
MOBILE ....
E-MAIL ....

Bulldog, Robert Morley

NAME...
....
ADDRESS ....
....
....
....
....
TEL ....
MOBILE ....
E-MAIL ....

NAME...
....
ADDRESS ....
....
....
....
....
TEL ....
MOBILE ....
E-MAIL ....

B

NAME...
....
ADDRESS ....
....
....
....
....
TEL ....
MOBILE ....
E-MAIL ....

NAME...
....
ADDRESS ....
....
....
....
....
TEL ....
MOBILE ....
E-MAIL ....

NAME...
....
ADDRESS ....
....
....
....
....
TEL ....
MOBILE ....
E-MAIL ....

NAME...
....
ADDRESS ....
....
....
....
....
TEL ....
MOBILE ....
E-MAIL ....

NAME...
....
ADDRESS ....
....
....
....
....
TEL ....
MOBILE ....
E-MAIL ....

NAME...
....
ADDRESS ....
....
....
....
....
TEL ....
MOBILE ....
E-MAIL ....

Jack Russell, David George Steell

NAME ....   NAME ....
....
ADDRESS ....   ADDRESS ....
....
....
....
....
TEL ....   TEL ....
MOBILE ....   MOBILE ....
E-MAIL ....   E-MAIL ....

C

Pointer, William Green

NAME..	NAME..
....	....
ADDRESS	ADDRESS ....
....	....
....	....
....	....
....	
TEL	TEL ....
MOBILE	MOBILE ....
E-MAIL	E-MAIL ....

C

NAME...

ADDRESS ....
....
....
....
....
TEL ....
MOBILE ....
E-MAIL ....

NAME...

ADDRESS ....
....
....
....
....
TEL ....
MOBILE ....
E-MAIL ....

NAME...

ADDRESS ....
....
....
....
....
TEL ....
MOBILE ....
E-MAIL ....

NAME...

ADDRESS ....
....
....
....
....
TEL ....
MOBILE ....
E-MAIL ....

NAME...

ADDRESS ....
....
....
....
....
TEL ....
MOBILE ....
E-MAIL ....

NAME...

ADDRESS ....
....
....
....
....
TEL ....
MOBILE ....
E-MAIL ....

C

NAME...
....
ADDRESS ....
....
....
....
....
TEL ....
MOBILE ....
E-MAIL ....

NAME...
....
ADDRESS ....
....
....
....
....
TEL ....
MOBILE ....
E-MAIL ....

NAME...
....
ADDRESS ....
....
....
....
....
TEL ....
MOBILE ....
E-MAIL ....

NAME...
....
ADDRESS ....
....
....
....
....
TEL ....
MOBILE ....
E-MAIL ....

NAME...
....
ADDRESS ....
....
....
....
....
TEL ....
MOBILE ....
E-MAIL ....

Greyhound and Poodle, Jean-Baptiste Oudry

Greyhound and King Charles Spaniel, John Frederick H⏐ ⏐⏐nr.

NAME..

....

ADDRESS ....

....

....

....

....

TEL ....

MOBILE ....

E-MAIL ....

⏐ME..

.. ..

A⏐⏐⏐⏐⏐⏐   ~ E

              ....

       ....

       ....

       ....

       ....

TEL ....

MOBILE⏐E.....................................

E-MAIL ⏐ ⏐ L...................................

D

Dachshund, Walter Harrowing

NAME...
....
ADDRESS ....
....
....
....
....
TEL ....
MOBILE ....
E-MAIL ....

NAME...
....
ADDRESS ....
....
....
....
....
TEL ....
MOBILE ....
E-MAIL ....

NAME..
....
ADDRESS ....
....
....
....
....
TEL ....
MOBILE ....
E-MAIL ....

NAME...
....
ADDRESS ....
....
....
....
....
TEL ....
MOBILE ....
E-MAIL ....

My Dachshund … is the best and gentlest and most reasonable and well-mannered, as well as the most beautiful. Henry James

D

NAME...

ADDRESS ....

....

....

TEL ....

MOBILE ....

E-MAIL ....

NAME...

ADDRESS ....

....

....

TEL ....

MOBILE ....

E-MAIL ....

Dachshunds, Ludwig Voltz

D

NAME..
....
ADDRESS ....
....
....
....
....
TEL ....
MOBILE ....
E-MAIL ....

NAME..
....
ADDRESS ....
....
....
....
....
TEL ....
MOBILE ....
E-MAIL ....

NAME..
....
ADDRESS ....
....
....
....
....
TEL ....
MOBILE ....
E-MAIL ....

NAME..
....
ADDRESS ....
....
....
....
....
TEL ....
MOBILE ....
E-MAIL ....

Dachshund, Maud Earl

NAME..
....
ADDRESS ....
....
....
....
....
TEL ....
MOBILE ....
E-MAIL ....

Pomeranian, Horatio Henry Couldery

NAME...

....

AI)RESS ....

..   ..

.   ...

          ....

          ....

    :L ....

   OBILE ....

   -MAIL ....

NAME...

....

ADDRESS ....

....

....

....

....

TEL ....

MOBILE ....

E-MAIL ....

NAME...

....

ADDRESS ....

....

....

....

....

TEL ....

MOBILE ....

E-MAIL ....

NAME...

....

ADDRESS ....

....

....

....

....

TEL ....

MOBILE ....

E-MAIL ....

E

NAME...
....
ADDRESS ....
....
....
....
....
TEL ....
MOBILE ....
E-MAIL ....

NAME...
....
ADDRESS ....
....
....
....
....
TEL ....
MOBILE ....
E-MAIL ....

NAME...
....
ADDRESS ....
....
....
....
....
TEL ....
MOBILE ....
E-MAIL ....

NAME...
....
ADDRESS ....
....
....
....
....
TEL ....
MOBILE ....
E-MAIL ....

NAME...
....
ADDRESS ....
....
....
....
....
TEL ....
MOBILE ....
E-MAIL ....

NAME...
....
ADDRESS ....
....
....
....
....
TEL ....
MOBILE ....
E-MAIL ....

E

NAME...

....

ADDRESS ....

....

....

....

....

TEL ....

MOBILE ....

E-MAIL ....

NAME...

....

ADDRESS ....

....

....

....

....

TEL ....

MOBILE ....

E-MAIL ....

Scottish Terrier, J. Fitz Marshall

NAME...

....

ADDRESS ....

....

....

....

....

TEL ....

MOBILE ....

E-MAIL ....

NAME...

....

ADDRESS ....

....

....

....

....

TEL ....

MOBILE ....

E-MAIL ....

E

NAME..
....
ADDRESS ....
....
....
....
....
TEL ....
MOBILE ....
E-MAIL ....

NAME..
....
ADDRESS ....
....
....
....
....
TEL ....
MOBILE ....
E-MAIL ....

NAME..
....
ADDRESS ....
....
....
....
....
TEL ....
MOBILE ....
E-MAIL ....

NAME..
....
ADDRESS ....
....
....
....
....
TEL ....
MOBILE ....
E-MAIL ....

NAME..
....
ADDRESS ....
....
....
....
....
TEL ....
MOBILE ....
E-MAIL ....

NAME..
....
ADDRESS ....
....
....
....
....
TEL ....
MOBILE ....
E-MAIL ....

Not the least hard thing to bear when they go away from us, these quiet friends, is that they carry away with them so many years of our own lives.
John Galsworthy

E

NAME ....

....

ADDRESS ....

....

....

....

....

TEL ....

MOBILE ....

E-MAIL ....

NAME ....

....

ADDRESS ....

....

....

....

....

TEL ....

MOBILE ....

E-MAIL ....

Pomeranian, Horatio Henry Couldery

F

Pomeranian, Henry Crowther

NAME...

....

ADDRESS ....

....

....

....

....

TEL ....

MOBILE ....

E-MAIL ....

NAME...

....

ADDRESS ....

....

....

....

....

TEL ....

MOBILE ....

E-MAIL ....

F

NAME..

....

ADDRESS ....

....

....

....

....

TEL ....

MOBILE ....

E-MAIL ....

NAME..

....

ADDRESS ....

....

....

....

....

TEL ....

MOBILE ....

E-MAIL ....

NAME..

....

ADDRESS ....

....

....

....

....

TEL ....

MOBILE ....

E-MAIL ....

NAME..

....

ADDRESS ....

....

....

....

....

TEL ....

MOBILE ....

E-MAIL ....

NAME..

....

ADDRESS ....

....

....

....

....

TEL ....

MOBILE ....

E-MAIL ....

NAME..

....

ADDRESS ....

....

....

....

....

TEL ....

MOBILE ....

E-MAIL ....

F

Borzois, Maud Earl

NAME..

....

ADDRESS ....

....

....

....

....

TEL ....

MOBILE ....

E-MAIL ....

NAME..

....

ADDRESS ....

....

....

....

....

TEL ....

MOBILE ....

E-MAIL ....

F

NAME..

ADDRESS ....

....

....

....

....

TEL ....
MOBILE ....
E-MAIL ....

NAME..

ADDRESS ....

....

....

....

....

TEL ....
MOBILE ....
E-MAIL ....

NAME..

ADDRESS ....

....

....

....

....

TEL ....
MOBILE ....
E-MAIL ....

NAME..

ADDRESS ....

....

....

....

....

TEL ....
MOBILE ....
E-MAIL ....

NAME..

ADDRESS ....

....

....

....

....

TEL ....
MOBILE ....
E-MAIL ....

NAME..

ADDRESS ....

....

....

....

....

TEL ....
MOBILE ....
E-MAIL ....

F

NAME...
....
ADDRESS ....
....
....
....
....
TEL ....
MOBILE ....
E-MAIL ....

NAME...
....
ADDRESS ....
....
....
....
....
TEL ....
MOBILE ....
E-MAIL ....

NAME...
....
ADDRESS ....
....
....
....
....
TEL ....
MOBILE ....
E-MAIL ....

NAME...
....
ADDRESS ....
....
....
....
....
TEL ....
MOBILE ....
E-MAIL ....

NAME...
....
ADDRESS ....
....
....
....
....
TEL ....
MOBILE ....
E-MAIL ....

NAME...
....
ADDRESS ....
....
....
....
....
TEL ....
MOBILE ....
E-MAIL ....

Pekingese, Henry Crowther

NAME	NAME ....
....	....
ADDRESS	ADDRESS ....
....	....
....	....
....	....
....	....
TEL	TEL ....
MOBILE	MOBILE ....
E-MAIL	E-MAIL ....

G

NAME...
....
ADDRESS ....
....
....
....
....
TEL ....
MOBILE ....
E-MAIL ....

NAME...
....
ADDRESS ....
....
....
....
....
TEL ....
MOBILE ....
E-MAIL ....

NAME...
....
ADDRESS ....
....
....
....
....
TEL ....
MOBILE ....
E-MAIL ....

NAME...
....
ADDRESS ....
....
....
....
....
TEL ....
MOBILE ....
E-MAIL ....

NAME...
....
ADDRESS ....
....
....
....
....
TEL ....
MOBILE ....
E-MAIL ....

NAME...
....
ADDRESS ....
....
....
....
....
TEL ....
MOBILE ....
E-MAIL ....

G

NAME......................................
....
ADDRESS ....
....
....
....
....
TEL ....
MOBILE ....
E-MAIL ....

NAME......................................
....
ADDRESS ....
....
....
....
....
TEL ....
MOBILE ....
E-MAIL ....

NAME......................................
....
ADDRESS ....
....
....
....
....
TEL ....
MOBILE ....
E-MAIL ....

NAME......................................
....
ADDRESS ....
....
....
....
....
TEL ....
MOBILE ....
E-MAIL ....

Pekingese, William Walls

G

No matter how little money and how few possesions you own, having a dog makes you rich.
Louis Sabin

NAME...
....
ADDRESS ....
....
....
....
....
TEL ....
MOBILE ....
E-MAIL ....

NAME...
....
ADDRESS ....
....
....
....
....
TEL ....
MOBILE ....
E-MAIL ....

NAME...
....
ADDRESS ....
....
....
....
....
TEL ....
MOBILE ....
E-MAIL ....

NAME...
....
ADDRESS ....
....
....
....
....
TEL ....
MOBILE ....
E-MAIL ....

NAME...
....
ADDRESS ....
....
....
....
....
TEL ....
MOBILE ....
E-MAIL ....

NAME...
....
ADDRESS ....
....
....
....
....
TEL ....
MOBILE ....
E-MAIL ....

G

Collie, Edwin Douglas

NAME..

ADDRESS ....

....

....

....

....

TEL ....

MOBILE ....

E-MAIL ....

NAME..

ADDRESS ....

....

....

....

....

TEL ....

MOBILE ....

E-MAIL ....

G

Fox Terrier, George Earl

NAME...

ADDRESS ....

....

....

....

....

TEL ....

MOBILE ....

E-MAIL ....

NAME...

ADDRESS ....

....

....

....

....

TEL ....

MOBILE ....

E-MAIL ....

NAME...

....

ADDRESS ....

....

....

....

....

TEL ....

MOBILE ....

E-MAIL ....

NAME...

....

ADDRESS ....

....

....

....

....

TEL ....

MOBILE ....

E-MAIL ....

To look at Montmorency you would imagine that he was an angel sent upon the earth, for some reason withheld from mankind, in the shape of a small fox-terrier.
Jerome K. Jerome

NAME......................................

ADDRESS ....

....

....

....

....

TEL ....

MOBILE ....

E-MAIL ....

NAME......................................

ADDRESS ....

....

....

....

....

TEL ....

MOBILE ....

E-MAIL ....

NAME......................................

ADDRESS ....

....

....

....

....

TEL ....

MOBILE ....

E-MAIL ....

NAME......................................

ADDRESS ....

....

....

....

....

TEL ....

MOBILE ....

E-MAIL ....

NAME......................................

ADDRESS ....

....

....

....

....

TEL ....

MOBILE ....

E-MAIL ....

NAME......................................

ADDRESS ....

....

....

....

....

TEL ....

MOBILE ....

E-MAIL ....

H

NAME..
....
ADDRESS ....
....
....
....
....
TEL ....
MOBILE ....
E-MAIL ....

NAME..
....
ADDRESS ....
....
....
....
....
TEL ....
MOBILE ....
E-MAIL ....

NAME..
....
ADDRESS ....
....
....
....
....
TEL ....
MOBILE ....
E-MAIL ....

NAME..
....
ADDRESS ....
....
....
....
....
TEL ....
MOBILE ....
E-MAIL ....

NAME..
....
ADDRESS ....
....
....
....
....
TEL ....
MOBILE ....
E-MAIL ....

NAME..
....
ADDRESS ....
....
....
....
....
TEL ....
MOBILE ....
E-MAIL ....

Clumber Spaniels, Arthur Wardle

NAME...
....
ADDRESS ....
....
....
....
....
TEL ....
MOBILE ....
E-MAIL ....

NAME...
....
ADDRESS ....
....
....
....
....
TEL ....
MOBILE ....
E-MAIL ....

H

NAME......................................	NAME......................................
....	....
ADDRESS	ADDRESS ....
....	....
....	....
....	....
....	....
TEL	TEL ....
MOBILE	MOBILE ....
E-MAIL	E-MAIL ....

NAME......................................	NAME......................................
....	....
ADDRESS	ADDRESS ....
....	....
....	....
....	....
....	....
TEL	TEL ....
MOBILE	MOBILE ....
E-MAIL	E-MAIL ....

NAME......................................	NAME......................................
....	....
ADDRESS	ADDRESS ....
....	....
....	....
....	....
....	....
TEL	TEL ....
MOBILE	MOBILE ....
E-MAIL	E-MAIL ....

NAME..

ADDRESS ....

....

....

....

TEL ....

MOBILE ....

E-MAIL ....

NAME..

....

ADDRESS ....

....

....

....

TEL ....

MOBILE ....

E-MAIL ....

Terrier, Maud Earl

NAME..

ADDRESS ....

....

....

....

TEL ....

MOBILE ....

E-MAIL ....

NAME..

ADDRESS ....

....

....

....

TEL ....

MOBILE ....

E-MAIL ....

French Bulldog, Fred Sitzler

NAME...

ADDRESS ....

....

....

....

....

TEL ....
MOBILE ....
E-MAIL ....

NAME...

ADDRESS ....

....

....

....

....

TEL ....
MOBILE ....
E-MAIL ....

NAME...

....

ADDRESS ....

....

....

....

....

TEL ....
MOBILE ....
E-MAIL ....

NAME...

....

ADDRESS ....

....

....

....

....

TEL ....
MOBILE ....
E-MAIL ....

I

NAME..

ADDRESS ....

....

....

....

....

TEL ....
MOBILE ....
E-MAIL ....

NAME..

ADDRESS ....

....

....

....

....

TEL ....
MOBILE ....
E-MAIL ....

NAME..

ADDRESS ....

....

....

....

....

TEL ....
MOBILE ....
E-MAIL ....

NAME..

ADDRESS ....

....

....

....

....

TEL ....
MOBILE ....
E-MAIL ....

Smooth Fox Terriers, Maud Earl

I

NAME...
....
ADDRESS ....
....
....
....
....
TEL ....
MOBILE ....
E-MAIL ....

NAME...
....
ADDRESS ....
....
....
....
....
TEL ....
MOBILE ....
E-MAIL ....

NAME...
....
ADDRESS ....
....
....
....
....
TEL ....
MOBILE ....
E-MAIL ....

NAME...
....
ADDRESS ....
....
....
....
....
TEL ....
MOBILE ....
E-MAIL ....

NAME...
....
ADDRESS ....
....
....
....
....
TEL ....
MOBILE ....
E-MAIL ....

NAME...
....
ADDRESS ....
....
....
....
....
TEL ....
MOBILE ....
E-MAIL ....

J

NAME...

ADDRESS ....

....

....

....

....

TEL ....

MOBILE ....

E-MAIL ....

NAME...

ADDRESS ....

....

....

....

....

TEL ....

MOBILE ....

E-MAIL ....

NAME...

ADDRESS ....

....

....

....

....

TEL ....

MOBILE ....

E-MAIL ....

NAME...

ADDRESS ....

....

....

....

....

TEL ....

MOBILE ....

E-MAIL ....

Irish Terrier, John Emms

NAME...

ADDRESS ....

....

....

....

....

TEL ....

MOBILE ....

E-MAIL ....

J

NAME..

....

ADDRESS ....

....

....

....

....

TEL ....

MOBILE ....

E-MAIL ....

NAME..

....

ADDRESS ....

....

....

....

....

TEL ....

MOBILE ....

E-MAIL ....

Scottish Terriers, Lilian Cheviot

He was born in Bercy on the outskirts of Paris and trained in France, and while he knows a little poodle-English, he responds quickly only to commands in French. Otherwise he has to translate, and that slows him down. John Steinbeck

K

NAME..

....

ADDRESS ....

....

....

....

....

TEL ....

MOBILE ....

E-MAIL ....

NAME..

....

ADDRESS ....

....

....

....

....

TEL ....

MOBILE ....

E-MAIL ....

NAME..

....

ADDRESS ....

....

....

....

....

TEL ....

MOBILE ....

E-MAIL ....

NAME..

....

ADDRESS ....

....

....

....

....

TEL ....

MOBILE ....

E-MAIL ....

NAME..

....

ADDRESS ....

....

....

....

....

TEL ....

MOBILE ....

E-MAIL ....

NAME..

....

ADDRESS ....

....

....

....

....

TEL ....

MOBILE ....

E-MAIL ....

K

NAME.....................................
....
ADDRESS ....
....
....
....
....
TEL ....
MOBILE ....
E-MAIL ....

NAME.....................................
....
ADDRESS ....
....
....
....
....
TEL ....
MOBILE ....
E-MAIL ....

NAME.....................................
....
ADDRESS ....
....
....
....
....
TEL ....
MOBILE ....
E-MAIL ....

NAME.....................................
....
ADDRESS ....
....
....
....
....
TEL ....
MOBILE ....
E-MAIL ....

King Charles Spaniel, Samuel Spode

NAME.....................................
....
ADDRESS ....
....
....
....
....
TEL ....
MOBILE ....
E-MAIL ....

K

NAME..

....

ADDRESS ....

....

....

....

....

TEL ....

MOBILE ....

E-MAIL ....

NAME..

....

ADDRESS ....

....

....

....

....

TEL ....

MOBILE ....

E-MAIL ....

King Charles Spaniel, James Ward (attrib.)

NAME.. NAME..

....

ADDRESS .... ADDRESS ....

....

....

....

....

TEL .... TEL ....

MOBILE .... MOBILE ....

E-MAIL .... E-MAIL ....

L

King Charles Spaniel, Frederick Hall

NAME ....

....

ADDRESS ....

....

....

....

....

TEL ....

MOBILE ....

E-MAIL ....

NAME ....

....

ADDRESS ....

....

....

....

....

TEL ....

MOBILE ....

E-MAIL ....

NAME ....

....

ADDRESS ....

....

....

....

....

TEL ....

MOBILE ....

E-MAIL ....

NAME ....

....

ADDRESS ....

....

....

....

....

TEL ....

MOBILE ....

E-MAIL ....

NAME ....

....

ADDRESS ....

....

....

....

....

TEL ....

MOBILE ....

E-MAIL ....

L

NAME...

....

ADDRESS ....

....

....

....

....

TEL ....

MOBILE ....

E-MAIL ....

NAME...

....

ADDRESS ....

....

....

....

....

TEL ....

MOBILE ....

E-MAIL ....

Toy Spaniels, Adolphe Thomasse

L

NAME..

....

ADDRESS ....

....

....

....

....

TEL ....

MOBILE ....

E-MAIL ....

NAME..

....

ADDRESS ....

....

....

....

....

TEL ....

MOBILE ....

E-MAIL ....

NAME..

....

ADDRESS ....

....

....

....

....

TEL ....

MOBILE ....

E-MAIL ....

NAME..

....

ADDRESS ....

....

....

....

....

TEL ....

MOBILE ....

E-MAIL ....

'Highland Tod, Fox Hunter', Richard Ansdell

Otterhounds, Walter Hunt, Jnr.

NAME ....

ADDRESS ....

....

....

....

....

TEL ....

MOBILE ....

E-MAIL ....

NAME ....

....

ADDRESS ....

....

....

....

....

TEL ....

MOBILE ....

E-MAIL ....

M

Rough-Coated Beagle, Thomas Earl

NAME ....

ADDRESS ....

TEL ....
MOBILE ....
E-MAIL ....

NAME ....

ADDRESS ....

TEL ....
MOBILE ....
E-MAIL ....

NAME ....

ADDRESS ....

TEL ....
MOBILE ....
E-MAIL ....

NAME ....

ADDRESS ....

TEL ....
MOBILE ....
E-MAIL ....

NAME ....

ADDRESS ....

TEL ....
MOBILE ....
E-MAIL ....

M

NAME..

ADDRESS ....

....

....

....

....

TEL ....

MOBILE ....

E-MAIL ....

NAME..

ADDRESS ....

....

....

....

....

TEL ....

MOBILE ....

E-MAIL ....

NAME..

ADDRESS ....

....

....

....

....

TEL ....

MOBILE ....

E-MAIL ....

NAME..

ADDRESS ....

....

....

....

....

TEL ....

MOBILE ....

E-MAIL ....

NAME..

ADDRESS ....

....

....

....

....

TEL ....

MOBILE ....

E-MAIL ....

NAME..

ADDRESS ....

....

....

....

....

TEL ....

MOBILE ....

E-MAIL ....

M

Bloodhound, John Sargent Noble

NAME...
....
ADDRESS ....
....
....
....
....
TEL ....
MOBILE ....
E-MAIL ....

NAME...
....
ADDRESS ....
....
....
....
....
TEL ....
MOBILE ....
E-MAIL ....

NAME...
....
ADDRESS ....
....
....
....
....
TEL ....
MOBILE ....
E-MAIL ....

NAME...
....
ADDRESS ....
....
....
....
....
TEL ....
MOBILE ....
E-MAIL ....

NAME...
....
ADDRESS ....
....
....
....
....
TEL ....
MOBILE ....
E-MAIL ....

God created man; then seeing how weak he was, gave him the dog.
Alphonse Toussenel

NAME..

ADDRESS ....

TEL ....
MOBILE ....
E-MAIL ....

NAME..

ADDRESS ....

TEL ....
MOBILE ....
E-MAIL ....

Bloodhound, Reuben Ward Binks

M

NAME..
....
ADDRESS ....
....
....
....
....
TEL ....
MOBILE ....
E-MAIL ....

NAME..
....
ADDRESS ....
....
....
....
....
TEL ....
MOBILE ....
E-MAIL ....

NAME..
....
ADDRESS ....
....
....
....
....
TEL ....
MOBILE ....
E-MAIL ....

NAME..
....
ADDRESS ....
....
....
....
....
TEL ....
MOBILE ....
E-MAIL ....

NAME..
....
ADDRESS ....
....
....
....
....
TEL ....
MOBILE ....
E-MAIL ....

NAME..
....
ADDRESS ....
....
....
....
....
TEL ....
MOBILE ....
E-MAIL ....

I am his Highness' dog at Kew; pray tell me, sir, whose dog are you?
Alexander Pope

Newfoundland, Sir Edwin Landseer

NAME...

ADDRESS ....

....

....

....

....

TEL ....

MOBILE ....

E-MAIL ....

NAME...

ADDRESS ....

....

....

....

....

TEL ....

MOBILE ....

E-MAIL ....

N

NAME ....
....
ADDRESS ....
....
....
....
....
TEL ....
MOBILE ....
E-MAIL ....

NAME ....
....
ADDRESS ....
....
....
....
....
TEL ....
MOBILE ....
E-MAIL ....

NAME ....
....
ADDRESS ....
....
....
....
....
TEL ....
MOBILE ....
E-MAIL ....

NAME ....
....
ADDRESS ....
....
....
....
....
TEL ....
MOBILE ....
E-MAIL ....

NAME ....
....
ADDRESS ....
....
....
....
....
TEL ....
MOBILE ....
E-MAIL ....

NAME ....
....
ADDRESS ....
....
....
....
....
TEL ....
MOBILE ....
E-MAIL ....

Brothers and sisters, I bid you beware
Of giving your heart to a dog to tear.
Rudyard Kipling

O

NAME..

....

ADDRESS ....

....

....

....

....

TEL ....

MOBILE ....

E-MAIL ....

Maltese, George Earl

NAME..

....

ADDRESS ....

....

....

....

....

TEL ....

MOBILE ....

E-MAIL ....

NAME..

....

ADDRESS ....

....

....

....

....

TEL ....

MOBILE ....

E-MAIL ....

NAME..

....

ADDRESS ....

....

....

....

....

TEL ....

MOBILE ....

E-MAIL ....

NAME..

....

ADDRESS ....

....

....

....

....

TEL ....

MOBILE ....

E-MAIL ....

NAME..

ADDRESS ....
....
....
....
....
TEL ....
MOBILE ....
E-MAIL ....

NAME..

ADDRESS ....
....
....
....
....
TEL ....
MOBILE ....
E-MAIL ....

NAME..

ADDRESS ....
....
....
....
....
TEL ....
MOBILE ....
E-MAIL ....

NAME..

ADDRESS ....
....
....
....
....
TEL ....
MOBILE ....
E-MAIL ....

NAME..

ADDRESS ....
....
....
....
....
TEL ....
MOBILE ....
E-MAIL ....

NAME..

ADDRESS ....
....
....
....
....
TEL ....
MOBILE ....
E-MAIL ....

P

NAME...
....
ADDRESS ....
....
....
....
....
TEL ....
MOBILE ....
E-MAIL ....

NAME...
....
ADDRESS ....
....
....
....
....
TEL ....
MOBILE ....
E-MAIL ....

Pug and Terrier, John Sargent Noble

P

NAME...
....
ADDRESS ....
....
....
....
....
TEL ....
MOBILE ....
E-MAIL ....

NAME...
....
ADDRESS ....
....
....
....
....
TEL ....
MOBILE ....
E-MAIL ....

P

NAME..
....
ADDRESS ....
....
....
....
....
TEL ....
MOBILE ....
E-MAIL ....

NAME..
....
ADDRESS ....
....
....
....
....
TEL ....
MOBILE ....
E-MAIL ....

NAME..
....
ADDRESS ....
....
....
....
....
TEL ....
MOBILE ....
E-MAIL ....

NAME..
....
ADDRESS ....
....
....
....
....
TEL ....
MOBILE ....
E-MAIL ....

NAME..
....
ADDRESS ....
....
....
....
....
TEL ....
MOBILE ....
E-MAIL ....

NAME..
....
ADDRESS ....
....
....
....
....
TEL ....
MOBILE ....
E-MAIL ....

Papillon and Pug, Carl Steffeck

NAME...

....

ADDRESS ....

....

....

....

....

TEL ....

MOBILE ....

E-MAIL ....

NAME...

....

ADDRESS ....

....

....

....

....

TEL ....

MOBILE ....

E-MAIL ....

P

NAME.. NAME..

....

ADDRESS .... ADDRESS ....

....

....

....

....

TEL .... TEL ....

MOBILE .... MOBILE ....

E-MAIL .... E-MAIL ....

Papillon, Malcolm S. Tucker

P

NAME..
....
ADDRESS ....
....
....
....
....
TEL ....
MOBILE ....
E-MAIL ....

NAME..
....
ADDRESS ....
....
....
....
....
TEL ....
MOBILE ....
E-MAIL ....

NAME..
....
ADDRESS ....
....
....
....
....
TEL ....
MOBILE ....
E-MAIL ....

NAME..
....
ADDRESS ....
....
....
....
....
TEL ....
MOBILE ....
E-MAIL ....

NAME..
....
ADDRESS ....
....
....
....
....
TEL ....
MOBILE ....
E-MAIL ....

NAME..
....
ADDRESS ....
....
....
....
....
TEL ....
MOBILE ....
E-MAIL ....

NAME..

ADDRESS ....

....

....

....

....

TEL ....

MOBILE ....

E-MAIL ....

NAME..

ADDRESS ....

....

....

....

....

TEL ....

MOBILE ....

E-MAIL ....

NAME..

ADDRESS ....

....

....

....

....

TEL ....

MOBILE ....

E-MAIL ....

NAME..

ADDRESS ....

....

....

....

....

TEL ....

MOBILE ....

E-MAIL ....

NAME..

ADDRESS ....

....

....

....

....

TEL ....

MOBILE ....

E-MAIL ....

NAME..

ADDRESS ....

....

....

....

....

TEL ....

MOBILE ....

E-MAIL ....

Scottish Deerhounds, Conradijn Cunæus

NAME..

....

ADDRESS ....

....

....

....

....

TEL ....

MOBILE ....

E-MAIL ....

NAME..

....

ADDRESS ....

....

....

....

....

TEL ....

MOBILE ....

E-MAIL ....

R

NAME...

ADDRESS ....

TEL ....
MOBILE ....
E-MAIL ....

NAME...

ADDRESS ....

TEL ....
MOBILE ....
E-MAIL ....

NAME...

ADDRESS ....

TEL ....
MOBILE ....
E-MAIL ....

NAME...

ADDRESS ....

TEL ....
MOBILE ....
E-MAIL ....

NAME...

ADDRESS ....

TEL ....
MOBILE ....
E-MAIL ....

NAME...

ADDRESS ....

TEL ....
MOBILE ....
E-MAIL ....

R

NAME..

ADDRESS ....

....

....

....

....

TEL ....

MOBILE ....

E-MAIL ....

Scottish Deerhound, George Earl

NAME..

ADDRESS ....

....

....

....

....

TEL ....

MOBILE ....

E-MAIL ....

NAME..

ADDRESS ....

....

....

....

....

TEL ....

MOBILE ....

E-MAIL ....

NAME..

ADDRESS ....

....

....

....

....

TEL ....

MOBILE ....

E-MAIL ....

NAME..

ADDRESS ....

....

....

....

....

TEL ....

MOBILE ....

E-MAIL ....

R

NAME...
....
ADDRESS ....
....
....
....
....
TEL ....
MOBILE ....
E-MAIL ....

NAME...
....
ADDRESS ....
....
....
....
....
TEL ....
MOBILE ....
E-MAIL ....

NAME...
....
ADDRESS ....
....
....
....
....
TEL ....
MOBILE ....
E-MAIL ....

NAME...
....
ADDRESS ....
....
....
....
....
TEL ....
MOBILE ....
E-MAIL ....

NAME...
....
ADDRESS ....
....
....
....
....
TEL ....
MOBILE ....
E-MAIL ....

NAME...
....
ADDRESS ....
....
....
....
....
TEL ....
MOBILE ....
E-MAIL ....

NAME...

ADDRESS ....

TEL ....
MOBILE ....
E-MAIL ....

NAME...

ADDRESS ....

TEL ....
MOBILE ....
E-MAIL ....

NAME...

ADDRESS ....

TEL ....
MOBILE ....
E-MAIL ....

Field Spaniel, Maud Earl

NAME...

ADDRESS ....

TEL ....
MOBILE ....
E-MAIL ....

NAME...

ADDRESS ....

TEL ....
MOBILE ....
E-MAIL ....

S

NAME..
....
ADDRESS ....
....
....
....
....
TEL ....
MOBILE ....
E-MAIL ....

NAME..
....
ADDRESS ....
....
....
....
....
TEL ....
MOBILE ....
E-MAIL ....

NAME..
....
ADDRESS ....
....
....
....
....
TEL ....
MOBILE ....
E-MAIL ....

NAME..
....
ADDRESS ....
....
....
....
....
TEL ....
MOBILE ....
E-MAIL ....

NAME..
....
ADDRESS ....
....
....
....
....
TEL ....
MOBILE ....
E-MAIL ....

NAME..
....
ADDRESS ....
....
....
....
....
TEL ....
MOBILE ....
E-MAIL ....

T

NAME ....
....
ADDRESS ....
....
....
....
....
TEL ....
MOBILE ....
E-MAIL ....

NAME ....
....
ADDRESS ....
....
....
....
....
TEL ....
MOBILE ....
E-MAIL ....

NAME ....
....
ADDRESS ....
....
....
....
....
TEL ....
MOBILE ....
E-MAIL ....

NAME ....
....
ADDRESS ....
....
....
....
....
TEL ....
MOBILE ....
E-MAIL ....

NAME ....
....
ADDRESS ....
....
....
....
....
TEL ....
MOBILE ....
E-MAIL ....

NAME ....
....
ADDRESS ....
....
....
....
....
TEL ....
MOBILE ....
E-MAIL ....

T

T

Gordon Setter, Fr

NAME...

ADDRESS ....

....

....

....

....

TEL ....

MOBILE ....

E-MAIL ....

NAME...

ADDRESS ....

....

....

....

....

....

....

....

NAME...

ADDRESS ....

....

....

....

....

TEL ....

MOBILE ....

E-MAIL ....

TEL ....

MOBILE ....

E-MAIL ....

T

NAME..

ADDRESS ....
....
....
....
....

TEL ....
MOBILE ....
E-MAIL ....

NAME..

ADDRESS ....
....
....
....
....

TEL ....
MOBILE ....
E-MAIL ....

NAME..

ADDRESS ....
....
....
....
....

TEL ....
MOBILE ....
E-MAIL ....

NAME..

ADDRESS ....
....
....
....
....

TEL ....
MOBILE ....
E-MAIL ....

NAME..

ADDRESS ....
....
....
....
....

TEL ....
MOBILE ....
E-MAIL ....

NAME..

ADDRESS ....
....
....
....
....

TEL ....
MOBILE ....
E-MAIL ....

T

NAME...
....
ADDRESS ....
....
....
....
....
TEL ....
MOBILE ....
E-MAIL ....

NAME...
....
ADDRESS ....
....
....
....
....
TEL ....
MOBILE ....
E-MAIL ....

NAME...
....
ADDRESS ....
....
....
....
....
TEL ....
MOBILE ....
E-MAIL ....

NAME...
....
ADDRESS ....
....
....
....
....
TEL ....
MOBILE ....
E-MAIL ....

NAME...
....
ADDRESS ....
....
....
....
....
TEL ....
MOBILE ....
E-MAIL ....

NAME...
....
ADDRESS ....
....
....
....
....
TEL ....
MOBILE ....
E-MAIL ....

T

English Setter and Gordon Setter, William Arnold Woodhouse

NAME..
....
ADDRESS ....
....
....
....
....
TEL ....
MOBILE ....
E-MAIL ....

NAME..
....
ADDRESS ....
....
....
....
....
TEL ....
MOBILE ....
E-MAIL ....

T

NAME...
....
ADDRESS ....
....
....
....
....
TEL ....
MOBILE ....
E-MAIL ....

NAME...
....
ADDRESS ....
....
....
....
....
TEL ....
MOBILE ....
E-MAIL ....

NAME...
....
ADDRESS ....
....
....
....
....
TEL ....
MOBILE ....
E-MAIL ....

NAME...
....
ADDRESS ....
....
....
....
....
TEL ....
MOBILE ....
E-MAIL ....

King Charles Spaniels,
Alexander Pope

T

NAME...
....
ADDRESS ....
....
....
....
....
TEL ....
MOBILE ....
E-MAIL ....

NAME...
....
ADDRESS ....
....
....
....
....
TEL ....
MOBILE ....
E-MAIL ....

NAME...
....
ADDRESS ....
....
....
....
....
TEL ....
MOBILE ....
E-MAIL ....

NAME...
....
ADDRESS ....
....
....
....
....
TEL ....
MOBILE ....
E-MAIL ....

T

NAME...

....

ADDRESS ....

....

....

....

....

TEL ....

MOBILE ....

E-MAIL ....

NAME...

....

ADDRESS ....

....

....

....

....

TEL ....

MOBILE ....

E-MAIL ....

NAME...

....

ADDRESS ....

....

....

....

....

TEL ....

MOBILE ....

E-MAIL ....

NAME...

....

ADDRESS ....

....

....

....

....

TEL ....

MOBILE ....

E-MAIL ....

NAME...

....

ADDRESS ....

....

....

....

....

TEL ....

MOBILE ....

E-MAIL ....

NAME..

ADDRESS ....

....

....

....

....

TEL ....

MOBILE ....

E-MAIL ....

NAME..

ADDRESS ....

....

....

....

....

TEL ....

MOBILE ....

E-MAIL ....

NAME..

ADDRESS ....

....

....

....

....

TEL ....

MOBILE ....

E-MAIL ....

NAME..

ADDRESS ....

....

....

....

....

TEL ....

MOBILE ....

E-MAIL ....

Opposite and above: Fox Terrier and Manchester
Terrier, Briton Riviere

U

NAME...
....
ADDRESS ....
....
....
....
....
TEL ....
MOBILE ....
E-MAIL ....

NAME...
....
ADDRESS ....
....
....
....
....
TEL ....
MOBILE ....
E-MAIL ....

NAME...
....
ADDRESS ....
....
....
....
....
TEL ....
MOBILE ....
E-MAIL ....

NAME...
....
ADDRESS ....
....
....
....
....
TEL ....
MOBILE ....
E-MAIL ....

NAME...
....
ADDRESS ....
....
....
....
....
TEL ....
MOBILE ....
E-MAIL ....

NAME...
....
ADDRESS ....
....
....
....
....
TEL ....
MOBILE ....
E-MAIL ....

Money will buy you a pretty good dog, but it won't buy the wag of his tail. Henry Wheeler Shaw

NAME..

....

ADDRESS ....

....

....

....

....

TEL ....

MOBILE ....

E-MAIL ....

NAME..

....

ADDRESS ....

....

....

....

....

TEL ....

MOBILE ....

E-MAIL ....

Fox Terrier, John Emms

U

NAME..
....
ADDRESS ....
....
....
....
....
TEL ....
MOBILE ....
E-MAIL ....

NAME..
....
ADDRESS ....
....
....
....
....
TEL ....
MOBILE ....
E-MAIL ....

NAME..
....
ADDRESS ....
....
....
....
....
TEL ....
MOBILE ....
E-MAIL ....

NAME..
....
ADDRESS ....
....
....
....
....
TEL ....
MOBILE ....
E-MAIL ....

NAME..
....
ADDRESS ....
....
....
....
....
TEL ....
MOBILE ....
E-MAIL ....

NAME..
....
ADDRESS ....
....
....
....
....
TEL ....
MOBILE ....
E-MAIL ....

Fox Terrier, Robert Morley

NAME..

....

ADDRESS ....

....

....

....

....

TEL ....

MOBILE ....

E-MAIL ....

NAME..

....

ADDRESS ....

....

....

....

....

TEL ....

MOBILE ....

E-MAIL ....

V

Corgis, Arthur Wardle

NAME..

ADDRESS ....

....

....

....

....

TEL ....

MOBILE ....

E-MAIL ....

NAME..

....

ADDRESS ....

....

....

....

....

TEL ....

MOBILE ....

E-MAIL ....

NAME..

....

ADDRESS ....

....

....

....

....

TEL ....

MOBILE ....

E-MAIL ....

NAME..

....

ADDRESS ....

....

....

....

....

TEL ....

MOBILE ....

E-MAIL ....

V

NAME..

ADDRESS ....

TEL ....
MOBILE ....
E-MAIL ....

NAME..

ADDRESS ....

TEL ....
MOBILE ....
E-MAIL ....

NAME..

ADDRESS ....

TEL ....
MOBILE ....
E-MAIL ....

NAME..

ADDRESS ....

TEL ....
MOBILE ....
E-MAIL ....

NAME..

ADDRESS ....

TEL ....
MOBILE ....
E-MAIL ....

NAME..

ADDRESS ....

TEL ....
MOBILE ....
E-MAIL ....

Labradors, R. Ward Binks

NAME..
....
ADDRESS ....
....
....
....
....
TEL ....
MOBILE ....
E-MAIL ....

NAME..
....
ADDRESS ....
....
....
....
....
TEL ....
MOBILE ....
E-MAIL ....

NAME..
....
ADDRESS ....
....
....
....
....
TEL ....
MOBILE ....
E-MAIL ....

NAME..
....
ADDRESS ....
....
....
....
....
TEL ....
MOBILE ....
E-MAIL ....

NAME..

....

ADDRESS ....

....

....

....

....

TEL ....

MOBILE ....

E-MAIL ....

NAME..

....

ADDRESS ....

....

....

....

....

TEL ....

MOBILE ....

E-MAIL ....

NAME..

....

ADDRESS ....

....

....

....

....

TEL ....

MOBILE ....

E-MAIL ....

NAME..

....

ADDRESS ....

....

....

....

....

TEL ....

MOBILE ....

E-MAIL ....

NAME..

....

ADDRESS ....

....

....

....

....

TEL ....

MOBILE ....

E-MAIL ....

NAME..

....

ADDRESS ....

....

....

....

....

TEL ....

MOBILE ....

E-MAIL ....

NAME...

ADDRESS ....

....

....

....

....

TEL ....

MOBILE ....

E-MAIL ....

NAME...

ADDRESS ....

....

....

....

....

TEL ....

MOBILE ....

E-MAIL ....

NAME...

ADDRESS ....

....

....

....

....

TEL ....

MOBILE ....

E-MAIL ....

NAME...

ADDRESS ....

....

....

....

....

TEL ....

MOBILE ....

E-MAIL ....

NAME...

ADDRESS ....

....

....

....

....

TEL ....

MOBILE ....

E-MAIL ....

NAME...

ADDRESS ....

....

....

....

....

TEL ....

MOBILE ....

E-MAIL ....

NAME..

ADDRESS ....

....

....

....

....

TEL ....

MOBILE ....

E-MAIL ....

NAME..

ADDRESS ....

....

....

....

....

TEL ....

MOBILE ....

E-MAIL ....

King Charles Spaniel, Arthur Fitzwilliam Tait

NAME..

ADDRESS ....

....

....

....

....

TEL ....

MOBILE ....

E-MAIL ....

NAME..

ADDRESS ....

....

....

....

....

TEL ....

MOBILE ....

E-MAIL ....

NAME..

ADDRESS ....

....

....

....

....

TEL ....

MOBILE ....

E-MAIL ....

NAME..

ADDRESS...
....
....
....
....
TEL...
MOBILE...
E-MAIL...

NAME..
....
ADDRESS...
....
....
....
....
TEL...
MOBILE...
E-MAIL...

NAME..
....
ADDRESS...
....
....
....
....
TEL...
MOBILE...
E-MAIL...

NAME..
....
ADDRESS...
....
....
....
....
TEL...
MOBILE...
E-MAIL...

NAME..
....
ADDRESS...
....
....
....
....
TEL...
MOBILE...
E-MAIL...

NAME..
....
ADDRESS...
....
....
....
....
TEL...
MOBILE...
E-MAIL...

NAME...
....
ADDRESS ....
....
....
....
....
TEL ....
MOBILE ....
E-MAIL ....

Dalmatian, Gustav Muss-Arnolt

NAME...
....
ADDRESS ....
....
....
....
....
TEL ....
MOBILE ....
E-MAIL ....

NAME...
....
ADDRESS ....
....
....
....
....
TEL ....
MOBILE ....
E-MAIL ....

NAME...
....
ADDRESS ....
....
....
....
....
TEL ....
MOBILE ....
E-MAIL ....

NAME...
....
ADDRESS ....
....
....
....
....
TEL ....
MOBILE ....
E-MAIL ....

NAME ....

....

ADDRESS ....

....

....

....

....

TEL ....

MOBILE ....

E-MAIL ....

NAME ....

....

ADDRESS ....

....

....

....

....

TEL ....

MOBILE ....

E-MAIL ....

NAME ....

....

ADDRESS ....

....

....

....

....

TEL ....

MOBILE ....

E-MAIL ....

NAME ....

....

ADDRESS ....

....

....

....

....

TEL ....

MOBILE ....

E-MAIL ....

NAME ....

....

ADDRESS ....

....

....

....

....

TEL ....

MOBILE ....

E-MAIL ....

NAME ....

....

ADDRESS ....

....

....

....

....

TEL ....

MOBILE ....

E-MAIL ....

Poodles always listen attentively while being scolded, looking innocent, bewildered, and misunderstood. James Thurber

X

NAME..

....

ADDRESS ....

....

....

....

....

TEL ....

MOBILE ....

E-MAIL ....

NAME..

....

ADDRESS ....

....

....

....

TEL ....

MOBILE ....

E-MAIL ....

Black Standard Poodle, Maud Earl

NAME..

....

ADDRESS ....

....

....

....

....

TEL ....

MOBILE ....

E-MAIL ....

NAME..

....

ADDRESS ....

....

....

....

....

TEL ....

MOBILE ....

E-MAIL ....

X

Y

NAME...
....
ADDRESS ....
....
....
....
....
TEL ....
MOBILE ....
E-MAIL ....

NAME...
....
ADDRESS ....
....
....
....
....
TEL ....
MOBILE ....
E-MAIL ....

NAME...
....
ADDRESS ....
....
....
....
....
TEL ....
MOBILE ....
E-MAIL ....

NAME...
....
ADDRESS ....
....
....
....
....
TEL ....
MOBILE ....
E-MAIL ....

NAME...
....
ADDRESS ....
....
....
....
....
TEL ....
MOBILE ....
E-MAIL ....

NAME...
....
ADDRESS ....
....
....
....
....
TEL ....
MOBILE ....
E-MAIL ....

'Left in Charge', William Henry Hamilton Trood

NAME...	NAME...
....	....
ADDRESS	ADDRESS ....
....	....
....	....
....	....
....	....
TEL	TEL ....
MOBILE	MOBILE ....
E-MAIL	E-MAIL ....

Y

NAME...
....
ADDRESS ....
....
....
....
....
TEL ....
MOBILE ....
E-MAIL ....

NAME...
....
ADDRESS ....
....
....
....
....
TEL ....
MOBILE ....
E-MAIL ....

NAME...
....
ADDRESS ....
....
....
....
....
TEL ....
MOBILE ....
E-MAIL ....

NAME...
....
ADDRESS ....
....
....
....
....
TEL ....
MOBILE ....
E-MAIL ....

NAME...
....
ADDRESS ....
....
....
....
....
TEL ....
MOBILE ....
E-MAIL ....

NAME...
....
ADDRESS ....
....
....
....
....
TEL ....
MOBILE ....
E-MAIL ....

Clumber Spaniel, Edwin Megargee

NAME...

ADDRESS ....

....

....

....

....

TEL ....

MOBILE ....

E-MAIL ....

NAME...

ADDRESS ....

....

....

....

....

TEL ....

MOBILE ....

E-MAIL ....

Z

NAME......................................
....
ADDRESS ....
....
....
....
....
TEL ....
MOBILE ....
E-MAIL ....

NAME......................................
....
ADDRESS ....
....
....
....
....
TEL ....
MOBILE ....
E-MAIL ....

NAME......................................
....
ADDRESS ....
....
....
....
....
TEL ....
MOBILE ....
E-MAIL ....

NAME......................................
....
ADDRESS ....
....
....
....
....
TEL ....
MOBILE ....
E-MAIL ....

NAME......................................
....
ADDRESS ....
....
....
....
....
TEL ....
MOBILE ....
E-MAIL ....

NAME......................................
....
ADDRESS ....
....
....
....
....
TEL ....
MOBILE ....
E-MAIL ....